REVERENT FLORA

REVERENT FLORA

THE ARABIAN DESERT'S BOTANICAL BOUNTY

POEMS BY DIANA WOODCOCK

SHANTI ARTS PUBLISHING

BRUNSWICK, MAINE

Published by Shanti Arts Publishing

Designed by Shanti Arts Designs

Cover image by Maha Mounir Akl, *The Stars and the Trees Bow Down*
(Qur'an 55:6), 2016; used with permission of the artist

Interior images by Charles Bleick and used with his permission

Scripture quotations marked (KJV) are taken from the KING JAMES
VERSION, public domain.

Scripture quotation (p. 101) is from the ESV® Bible (The Holy Bible,
English Standard Version®), © 2001 by Crossway, a publishing ministry of
Good News Publishers. Used by permission. All rights reserved.

Shanti Arts LLC
193 Hillside Road
Brunswick, Maine 04011
shantiarts.com

Printed in the United States of America

ISBN: 978-1-962082-48-8 (softcover)

Library of Congress Control Number: 2024952360

For Ali Sharif, Wildflower Expert

Contents

The Twenty-Two Most Mentioned Plants in the Qur'an

Epilogue

Acknowledgments

The author extends her gratitude to the editors of the following journals, in which some of these poems first appeared, at times in slightly different versions.

American Chordata: "Qur'anic Botanic Garden"

Avocet: "The Hardy Ones"; "Plantain Family" (as "Desert Ecology 47: *Plantaginaceae*"); and "Snapdragons and Black Mangroves" (as "Desert Ecology 45: *Scrophulariaceae* and *Acanthaceae*")

Cactus Heart: "Landforms" (as "Desert Ecology One: Landforms") and "Rocky Ridges" (as "Desert Ecology 2: Rocky Ridges")

Conservation and Sustainable Use of Wild Plant Diversity (Orthodox Academy of Crete Publications, 2011): "Broomrape Family" (as "Desert Ecology 46: *Orobanchaceae*"); "Carrot Family" (as "Desert Ecology 38-*Umbelliferae*"; "For Ali Sharif, Wildflower Expert"; "Jointfirs" (as "Desert Ecology 14: *Gymnospermae* Ephedra"); "Mint and Nightshade Families" (as "Desert Ecology 44: *Lamiaceae* and *Solanaceae*"); "Snapdragons and Black Mangroves" (as "Desert Ecology 45—*Scrophulariaceae* and *Acanthaceae*"; and "Wildflowers Over the Sand-sea."

Crab Creek Review: "Desert Squash and Red Thumbs" (as "Desert Ecology 37: Desert Squash and Red Thumbs")

Ellipsis . . . Literature and Art: "Bitter Apples" (as "*Citrullus Colocynthis*")

Journal of Medicinal Plant Conservation, 2024: United Plant Savers: "Garlic" and "Ginger"

Living City: "Manna"

The Missing Slate: "*Wadis* and Runnels" (as "Desert Ecology Lesson 3: Landforms—*Wadis* and Runnels")

Nimrod International Journal: "Carrot Family" (as "Desert Ecology 38: *Umbelliferae*") and "True Grasses" (as "Desert Ecology 52: *Gramineae*")

Off the Coast: "Between Mallows and Rock-roses" (as "Desert Ecology Lesson 35: *Malvaceae* and *Cistaceae*"); "The Caltrop Family" (as "Desert Ecology Lesson 31: *Zygophyllaceae*"); "Daisy Family" (as "Desert Ecology Lesson 48: *Compositae*"); "Iceplants" (as "Desert Ecology 20—*Aizoaceae*"); "Landforms" (as "Desert Ecology One: Landforms"); "Sabkhas" (as "Desert Ecology 4: Sabkhas"); "Sand Formations" (as "Desert Ecology 5: Sand Formations"); "Sand Primroses" (as "Desert Ecology 28: *Neuradaceae*"); and "Sedges" (as "Desert Ecology 57: *Cyperaceae*")

Petals in the Pan Anthology (Kind of a Hurricane Press, 2015): "Moonseeds and Desert Poppies" (as "Desert Ecology Lesson 24: *Menispermaceae* and *Papaveraceae*")

Pinyon Review: "Warning—Danger" (as "Desert Ecology Lesson 18: Warning—Danger")

Remembering Rainer Maria Rilke (anthology), Moonstone Press: "Fig"

Streetlight Magazine: "*Sabkhas*" (as "Desert Ecology 4: *Sabkhas*") and "The Hardy Ones"

Under the Spell of a Persian Nightingale (Word Poetry Books, 2015): "Bitter Apple" (as "*Citrullus Colocynthis*"); "Carrot Family" (as "Desert Ecology 38—*Umbelliferae*"); and "The Hardy Ones"

The Wayfarer: "Gourds and Parasitic Herbs Lacking Chlorophyll" (as "Desert Ecology Lesson 39: *Cucurbitaceau* and *Cynomoriaceau*")

Wild Flowers Anthology, Tiny Seed Press: "Leadworts and the Gentian Family"

Written River: "Buckthorns and Lindens" (as "Desert Ecology 34: *Rhamnaceae* and *Tiliaceae*")

The following poems appeared in the author's chapbook *Desert Ecology: Lessons and Visions* (Finishing Line Press, 2014): "Broomrape Family (*Orobanchaceae*)"; "Buckthorns and Lindens (*Rhamnaceae* and *Tiliaceae*)"; "For Ali Sharif, Wildflower Expert"; "Gum Arabic Tree (*Acacia*)"; "Jointfirs (*Gymnospermae Gnetopsida*); "Ephedrales, Mint and Nightshade Families (*Lamiaceae* and *Solanaceae*); "Once the Salubrious Winter Winds"; "Rocky Ridges, Sabkhas, Sand Formations, Sand primroses (*Neuradaceau*)"; "The Hardy Ones"; and "Wildflowers Over the Sand-Sea".

The following poems appeared in the author's chapbook *Tamed by the Desert* (Finishing Line Press, 2013): "Carrot Family (*Umbelliferae*)"; "Iceplants (*Aizoaceae*)"; "Landforms, Plantain Family (*Plantaginacceae*)"; "Sedges (*Cyperaceae*)"; "Snapdragons and Black Mangroves (*Scrophulariaceae* and *Acanthaceae*)"; "True Grasses (*Gramineae*)."

The author would like to thank Virginia Commonwealth University and the Faculty Research Grant Committee of VCUarts Qatar for a 2013 Presidential Research Quest Fund (PeRQ Fund) Award, which provided financial support and allowed me the time and resources for conducting research, writing, and revising these poems. Also, special thanks to the dedicated people working at Qatar's Qur'anic Botanic Garden: Fatima Bint Saleh Al-Khulaifi, Mohamed M. Hassona, and Ahmed E. El Gharib; as well as to my diligent research assistants in Qatar: Nimrah Kabiruddin and Ayaz Asadov. And for the exhilarating expeditions out into the desert, I am indebted to my desert wildflower expert guide, Ali Sharif, and co-explorers Fay Gotting and Susan Madzia.

The Plants and the Trees bow down.

—Qur'an 55:6

Full many a flow'r is born to blush unseen,
And waste its sweetness on the desert air.

—Thomas Gray, "Elegy Written
in a Country Churchyard"

Prologue

Qur'anic Botanic Garden

Inauguration Day, September 2008

A sidra sapling is planted at the proposed site.
Around it will grow three hundred species—
local flora, the Qur'an's ninety, the Hadith's
fifty—mustard, saffron, pumpkin, henna,
pomegranate, to name a few. A garden

designed like a traditional quadripartite—
four quarters, water canals, a central fountain—
to display over twenty-four hectares facts
from the Holy Book's one hundred and fifty
verses depicting divine flora.

Such diverse heads in concert: botanists,
phytochemists, engineers, architects,
Islamic scholars all agreeing on grapes,
figs, date palms, pomegranates finally
at the eleventh hour of habitat loss,

oil spills, inadequate livestock management.
Plan well, dear experts: *wadis*, *baadiya*,
rodats, oases, sunken flower-beds,
gulistans, *bustans*, plants from the coast,
the hills and gravel plains, sandy terrain,

aquatic habitats (Inland Sea and *wadis*).
Don't forget the salt-tolerant halophytes.
Grace this modern metropolis with a space
for reverie, for desert mind to hear a unified
botanical voice rising out of primordial sand.

Don't dawdle. Be quick and firm
before one more species is lost. Lead us
into plant presence—not one of us as clever
as the cactus with its spikes and prickles,
the acacia with its knack for attracting

fine waterborne sediments—wisely folding
its petals by midday. Place before us
a date palm just as its fruit is ripening, beckoning
to the avian migrants. Don't delay.
Create for us today a holy botanic garden.

Let the sidra sapling grow up strong and straight—
a sacred *lote* tree—leading us into holy presence.
But may we protect the wild, as well—
the camel thorn for starters, for those
sure-footed ships of the desert to graze.

Islam and Ecology

The seven heavens and the earth and all therein declare
His glory: there is not a thing but celebrates His praise.
—Qur'an 17:44

The problem begins
with separation of science
from the sacred, religion
from the secular; with denial

nature comes from a higher,
holier realm. Once the gist
of vicegerency is misconstrued,
nature's screwed.

Only one way will save it—
relive its sacredness,
bear witness to these truths:
nature depicts like an icon

the Creator—reflects Paradise,
memories kept in the soul's depths;
divine grace, *barakah*, flows
through arteries of the natural

and cosmic world order.
At every chance we must—
above all at dawn and dusk—
make the fields and forests,

desert flats and mountain peaks,
sky and sea our libraries;
inquire of the crows
what all they know;

turn our faces sunflower-like
to the blaze every single hour
of our fleeting earthly sojourn
in perfect unity and praise.

The Landscape

Warning—Danger

You'll be tempted at first to stay out
of the desert, warned of its dangers,
put off by its sparseness. But the secret
lies in walking the middle path between

its desolation and its veracity, seeking in
deep drifted sand that tufted perennial grass
(good fodder for the grazers), *Hammada
elegans*[1]—stout unarmed shrub Bedouins

once used to scrub clean their clothes,
Cyperus conglomeratus[2] on the sides
of barchan dunes, *Rhanterium
epapposum*[3] grazed by camels,

even ephemeral growth of *Zygophylum
simplex*[4] in the man-made hollow on the grey-
brown plateau. The secret is to know
where and when to go: after heavy storms

when every *rodat* is flooded with run-off water.
Go to where there's continuous spillage,
discharge of sewage, where *Phragmites
australis*[5] grows densely, spreading widely.

---

1. *Haloxylon persicum/Haloxylon salicornicum; ghada, gadha,* and
   rimth (Arabic)
2. Perennial sedge or *thenda* (Arabic)
3. No common name; *arfaj* (Arabic)
4. Simple-leaved bean caper; *hureim* (Arabic)
5. Common reed; *gazab* and *ghab* (Arabic)

Later you can brave oil fields and abandoned farms,
muster courage to sit in the empty space
between spring and winter, wait for the rains
to fill up *wadis*, flood the plains, transform

bare ground till it is hallowed once more.
Go bravely, sniff reverently for a whiff of heaven.
Praise all the brave ones who've defied the severe
state of affairs, the parched desert surface.

Don't fear the desert's core; it's not the foe.
Beware the polluted city on its edge, grown hard
as a callous, spreading like a cancer; beware the men—
each with his phallus shrinking from poisons

he's unleashing into air and sea. Pity
the workers in sand-caked buildings that scrape
the sky. Pity yourself unless you escape
to seek out and praise the heart of the desert.

Landforms

Let's begin with the rocky
hamadas, the unfruitable:
hazm and *mistah*.

One very gently sloping,
the other perfectly flat, covered
with fragments from in situ—

too heavy for the wind
to disperse. Poor soil, yet
lichens thrive on the stones.

In the fissures between them:
Zygophyllum quatarense, that bean caper
solo-flowered at each node, satisfied

in gravelly habitat with thinnest veneer
of surface deposits (I would need so little);
Acacia tortilis, small umbrella-shaped shrub

completely unarmed, pale yellow-headed;
Lycium shawii, bristly rigid with its red berry,
affably flowering year-round.

Each of these three abundant
in rocky *hamadas*, reliable, increasing
vigorously like a densely textured lyric—-

unflinching—each one an explosion
in *hazm* and *mistah* as elating
as a comet shooting across the night sky,

signifying what is most exalted
in desert ecology, performing their deeds
of bravery as loyally as any patriotic national

for the land of her birth.
Hardy, yes, but yet a tenderness
cracking the desert's pavement

where humans prove too fragile
to survive. Each one a quiet protest
against man's trespass.

Wadis and Runnels

Dry season. *Wadis* and runnels stark.
Beside them, one desert lark linking
sky and earth, quenching its thirst
at the thorny salt wort, trilling
in the language of longing,
igniting the listener's desire.

The lark, in full light, takes flight,
and I the wandering pilgrim
watching—rootless and wingless—
wax envious. In the hilly terrain,
southwestern region, massive ridges
and elevations with low-lying long runnels

create *wadis* Galal, Dhiab, Al-Jah
with their bristlegrassforming
phytogenic mounds in the main channels,
their shrubs of *Acacia ehrenbergiana*
and *Lycium shawii*, their fine sediments
cracking after drying, or rolling into thin

clay crusts like Pepperidge Farm's Pirouette
rolled wafers. Long runnels: some
dissecting desert pavement on limestone
Miocene ridgetops; some lying at low levels
between elevated *hamada* ridges;
others draining the plateau

(every pilgrim should know)—
their downstreams meandering westward.
Then, short narrow runnels dissecting
the ridges' gentle slopes, and runnels cutting
backwards confined to the Miocene ridges,
result of erosion, disintegration—

fine rock detritus on which grow
Acacia ehrenbergiana and *Pennisetum*
divisum, and on the wind-deposited sand,
Panicum turgidum. These *wadis*
and runnels, like the Spirit's messengers,
offer hope—encourage patience and faith—

word become runnel through which
life-giving water eventually will flow
across this span of arid land that I,
a welcomed pilgrim, feel I've known forever.
Peace be to dry, expectant *wadis*
and runnels winding

through desolate yet ultimate—

once the rains come—

blessed space.

Sabkhas

That night, after a day spent
on the coastal margins,
I dreamt I was a *sabkha* gently emerging

from the sea, displaying my fine silt
and calcareous sands like a proud weaver
of silk carpets and *kalims*.

I showcased my mangroves—
Avicennia marina—and my halo-
phytic plant communities:

glaucous glasswort,
sea rush, mangrove grass.
Mobile dunes encroached on me,

confining my vegetation to the lower level
between the cusps of coalesced dunes.
I glistened in the harsh sun,

gypsum crystals adorning me.
My silt and sands spread out
between sea and cracked earth

of packed desert pavement.
I proved a moist treasure trove
for slender-billed gulls,

whimbrels, sandpipers and crabs.
But whose waste was seeping
into my heart? Oblivious,

a wading little stint before day
was spent came to peck about my
mudflats, picking at plastic bags

and other junk,
taking just enough
to sustain it.

Rocky Ridges

Rocky mushroom-shaped outcroppings
grace the plant-poor Dukhan—Umm Bab Ridge.
Yet where sand accumulates in depressions,
thumam and harm abound.

Like talismans, they ward off fear,
declaring the nobility and grandeur
of rocky ridges, the tenacity
of the desert's deceptive simplicity,

the depth of each plant's quest
for what will sustain it, each one
a model of botanic integrity defying
the elements, gleaning from parched soil

enough sustenance to thrive,
each one offering hope for redemption,
a reason for reverence, gratitude.
Rocky ridges summon ancient stones,

advise the pilgrim to recall who
journeyed here before her, remind her
the desert merits affection—each plant
that's dug in its heels a simple yet complex

astonishment, a radiant testament.[1]

---

1. Refers to Qur'an 15:19, which states: "Earth was created in perfect balance."

Sand Formations

If you follow sand formations, you will find
barchans and dune fields, surface sands
and sand deposits in depressions
(read them like Turkish coffee grounds

in the bottom of your cup),
are prolific prophets—masters
of the divine sciences,
assuring you all shall be well,

even as the northwesterly wind
whittles away at them. Let yourself move
over surface sands like that prevailing
shamal. Be covered by aeolian grits

derived from the coast. Pace yourself
like those grains, advancing in leaps
to form thin sheets, humble hummocks,
barchan dunes, finally fields of serious sand.

Don't fear, the prophets of surface sands
advise, being thin and uneven,
trapped in crevices between rocks.
Note how sparse cover is enough

for bean caper and incense grass.
Sand deposits in depressions,
wadis and runnels say it's all about
depth and texture of sediments,

pointing to their denser plant cover—
Hammada elegans and *Panicum*
turgidum. Learn from the barchans—
those crescentic dunes known to play

                  lullabic tunes when the *shamal*
                strums them just right. Too mobile,
              they do not favor flora growing
            on their bodies, save for sedg

which thrives on their sides.
Barren, they coalesce and give themselves
to dune fields. Be a child
of the desert's sand formations

                    Though shadowed by death,
              they link the faithful to all that is
          illimitable and unknown, fleetingly
            saving us from rising waters.

You, dear pilgrim of the desert,
enter the councils of sand formations.
As grains rearrange themselves
at the hand of the *shamal*, you'll hear

            your name called in a shadowy language
               as you rise and fall with each
               world-contained grain. Winded,
              you'll linger on the barchan crest

like a child again at your mother's breast,
humbled, unwilling to let it all crumble.
As the pellucid surface of the desert
stretches out below you, you'll feel torn—

        one minute exultant, the next forlorn—
           sensing your life dwindling
              grain by grain, emptying
           into the vaster space of eternity.

Desert Flora Lessons

The Hardy Ones

As for those flowers cropping up where
least expected—hard-packed drifted sand,

shifting dunes, fossil corals,
among rocks and granite outcrops—

I would be so fool-hardy and daring,
delighting and surprising, a feast

for famished eyes under scorching sun.
Flowers that ignore pipelines,

oil rigs, keep-out signs,
country borders, undeterred

by endless sunny days, cloudless skies
over a hot subtropical desert.

Across the landscape—from flat terrain
to wavy hills to sand dunes—they bloom,

undaunted by wind-blown dust
and sandstorms, dry *wadis* and runnels,

course-textured arid soil.
Out of *rodat, sabkha,*

saline deposits, rocky lithosol,
sandy soil, they grow—ephemerals,

annuals, dwarf woody perennials
you need to see to believe:

field marigold sprouting from a rocky outcrop;
huwa and desert hyacinth pushing up

through hard-packed sand.
From a distance, you'll see nothing.

But go with anthophilous Ali,
and you'll swear he's pulling them

out of a hat—nothing there,
then just like that

he leans down and whispers,
Here. Cradled in a shell midden,

hidden: a rock-rose, *raqrouq*,
host of the treasured desert truffle, *kamah*.

Then he leads you further along—
there, suddenly, the desert campion;

and there, the caper plant,
Capparis spinosa.

Finally, you don't need him;
you've got the knack of it: you spot

the flora famous for shielding scorpions,
red arta. When finally returned home

to your well-kept walled-in garden,
you feel blasé about bougainvillea,

lantana, frangipani. You dream all night
of the hardy ones—steadfastly noble

in their earnest labors, convincing
anyone who'll kneel at their roots

a lifetime's not long enough
to seek out blooming sages

of the most desolate places.
You'll feel the only confessing

you need do is to desert wildflowers—
they with their infinite faith and powers

the ones who can call you back
to your rightful place

in the eternal scheme of things.

Jointfirs

Ephedra, *Gymnospermae gnetopsida*

And the servants of the Most Merciful are those who walk
upon the earth gently and humbly.   —Qur'an 25:63

Hazy autumn morning.
Season of mists. I tread gently
into the *rodat*, wild nature
under my feet, beads of dew
on leaves and limbs of sprawling
shrubs and woody climbers

like shrubby horsetail, with its filiform
leaves and nodes with short sheathes,
ascending wild jujube, its outspread
branches climbing winding
around its neighbors, offering itself
as a shield from foraging camels.

In this light-filled depression,
a *shamal* dispelling mist, I sit and wish,
gaining a singular sense of the camaraderie
of this plant community. If only
my neighbors could be as congenial.
I give thanks for the sprawlers and climbers,

all buds and tender shoots,
depressions sheltering and nurturing life—
defying the stereotype.
I kneel down to touch the place
where plant broke through hard-packed sand—
the earth giving birth.

Keeping still, I feel the goodwill
of ephedra embracing its neighbor,
sense my kinship as I seek neither
to destroy nor dominate—simply to emulate
its peaceful co-existence. Once
back home, sprawled out

on my tribal *kalim*, its arborescent
theme woven in thread, I'll dream
of being interleaved with *Ephedra foliata*—
protected from petroleum-laden wind
as a scarlet dragonfly rests on one
filiform leaf after its feast.

Iceplants

Aizoaceae

Take the prostrate herb *jafna*, *Aizoon*
canariense, for instance—seeming like a green
starfish flourishing in alluvial soil
in thin depressions along roadsides.
Or the succulent *ghasoul*—babies' toes—

its leaves glistening with blunt hairs.
Or slenderleaf iceplant—Egyptian fig marigold—
of dry salines and waste places.
Consider how each one endures, as if
its own angel's watching over it, tending it.

If you'll focus all your attention on just one,
you'll glimpse the deification of reality
as it becomes a presence to reckon with,
so vivid you'll sense it's making an appeal.
And before you can stop yourself,

you reply, What is it you need me to do?
Listen: Lean in closer. Voices from under
the hard-packed sand. Speak with them.
Become one with them. Rise up to be
transformed into an hermaphroditic flower,

simple perianth, fleshy calyx,
petaloid staminode, circumcissile
capsule of indehiscent fruit.
Realize you'll never survive alone.
You need *jafna*'s and *ghasoul*'s camaraderie.

You must speak for the iceplant
of slender leaf, must feel fire flashing
through every calyx tube, and letting go
of the terror, dare to act. Listen:
a lone Persian nightingale lamenting

in the sidra tree. Snap up each note. Hold it
close as if it's the last. Then release each one
to become drops of rain falling on each *jafna*,
ghasoul, Egyptian fig marigold rising
up from the desert's dry cracked floor.

Moonseeds and Desert Poppies

Menispermaceae and *Papaveraceae*

Mid-January: gray whales migrating
along North America's western coast.
Half a world away: shrubs twine and sway

in the desert breeze; a pack of camels
graze *gurdhi* as it climbs a jujube tree
at Al-Wabrah. And I wait,

April so far away, for that annual
herb *Papaver syriacum* to unfurl
its wide perse petals. While I wait,

two scarab beetles copulate.
A daytime moth sips from miniscule
white blossoms I would have missed

without its presence. Pouring a mint
elixir from my thermos, I settle
on the only available *jebel* around

to attend to the sound of one desert lark
singing its heart out to whomever will listen—
Allah its provision.[1]

---

1. Refers to Qur'an 11:6, which states, "…but that upon Allah is its
   provision, and He knows its place of dwelling and place of storage.
   All is in a clear register."

I stay, ecstatic to be far away
from the city's malls and traffic jams,
to be right where I am.

Though much too warm for January,
I throw myself into the fire and greening—
coaxed back from the edge of the cliff.

Finding solace among twining shrubs
and voices crooning ancient songs—
Persian bulbul, desert lark—

I am convinced yet again: silence
and the sloughing off of superfluous stuff
at the entrance to the desert's heart

are the only means to humility
and the peace of obscurity. Truth revealed:
sowing, not reaping, matters most.

To this, I drink a toast
to the smallest blossom opening
briefly, closing before midday,

to the climbing moonseeds
and the trusting of wild jujube
to take us all the way to heaven.

Sand Primroses (A Breath of Blessing)

Neuradaceae

At every turn, a choice to make—
to stay at work or wander out
into the desert on a solitary ramble.
Come November, I let sand primroses
tempt me away for one whole day.

What sets them apart:
peculiar fruit—hard,
discoid, spinose—seeds
retained in germination.

Take, for instance, sand buttons,
those creeping thorn roses: fruit clasped
collar-like around rootstocks,
the base of new and mature plants;
of prosperous augury[1]
they say in Arabia.

A gust of the *shamal* whitens
these prostrate herbs. Fragrance
of rain wafts over their southern
sandy terrain. Rattle of date palm
fronds like a sutra. A phalanx
of a vertebrate, foot perhaps
of a desert fox, lies beneath one.

---

1.   A line from a poem by Sufi poet Jamil Ibn Sa'dan

Tomentose or woolly herb.
I let myself fall asleep at the base
of one new plant, become a holy fool,
a dreamer, innocent of all charges
against me. Safe now with Neurada,
I can let the terror out.

Its sweet breathing a blessing
on the sandy habitat.
A still life of herb: seeds,
fruit, rootstock. I dare not
let even my shadow disturb it.

I leave the phalanx unfingered.

The Caltrop Family

Zygophyllaceae

Go sit in your cell, and it will teach you everything,
   Desert Father Abba Moses advises.
   But the caltrop family opposes his advice,

      takes this position: the xerophytes
   and halophytes have secrets to tell you;
      don't sit all alone in your cell;

      come out to sandy habitats for a spell,
   sit among fagonbushes and *Seetzenia lanata*,
      considering the life of herbs:

   how they flower and fruit in perfect poise
   and silence, their serenity to be envied.
      Sit humbly, tranquil and still,

      among *Fagonia indica*, watching
   stipular spines spread while calyxes persist.
      Note how *Seetzenia orientalis*,

      its sepals elongating into fruit,
   articulates the world's impermanence.
      Shave your head, change your name

   to Desert Herb; then take your preferred
   seat beside beancaper shrublets and annual
   succulents gracing rocky pebbly habitats—

the text of the five petals and five-
chambered ovaries of *harm* and *hureim*
like tanka sequences.

Throb of wild camels grazing herbs
and shrubs. Scent of rain on the *shamal*.
Jebels of bones. Recall the history

of the illustrious beancaper,
salvation to be found
in the varieties that abound.[1]

---

1.   Refers to Qur'an 67:3–4

Buckthorns and Lindens

Rhamnaceae and *Tiliaceae*

When all the world's bad news
has brought you down

rise up   go out to the *rodat*
depressions of loamy compact soil

where desert trees   shrubs woody
climbers flourish   and rejoice with them[1]

in sunlight and air   then
as the day goes   so let each care

seek out that red date
thorny shrub with almond-green

florets and orange berries
sidr its Qur'an-given name

find wild jute   that prostrate
perennial with tortuous branches

forming mats on compacted soil
look up from the flora

stark horizon   neither lofty pines
nor majestic maples   but at your feet

---

1.   Refers to Qur'an 17:44

a feast of herb   shrub
                         small tree

care for them as a form of prayer
commend their fecundity

consider buffalo thorns and lindens
as friends   then watch what happens

Between Mallows and Rock Roses

Malvaceae and *Cistaceae*

Try this: perch on a sandstone *jebel*

      soar in the space

between mallows and rock-roses

      in a place

devoid of man

      early February

Feast of Saint Brigit or Imbolic Day

      winter into spring

Hear the greening flowering desert

      calling you

summoning compassion

for ones bearing capsules

      splitting open along midribs

of modified leaves

      or dry fruit of indehiscent multiple carpels

Indian mallow

    Althaea ludwigii
cheeseweed common in depressions

      Reverence herbs   shrubs

      rock-roses   frostweeds

tendering calcareous rocks

and shallow depressions

    truffles

growing in alliance with some

Feel the desert tremble

    with floral presence

the accusing iridescent eye

    of the dragonfly

the *wadis* seeping

    From every shrub and herb
a sweet breathing

Sit in the space

between *Malva*

and *Cistace*
become the desert's *khalifah*[1]

ordained by black redstart

desert lark

gerbil and jird

as it stretches

before you

all

the universe

you need

all

you

need

_____

1. Refers to Qur'an 49:13

Desert Squash and Red Thumbs

Citrullus colocynthis and *Cynomorium coccineum*

No wonder at all *it was the desert,*
not the temple, that gave us the prophets.[1]

When I do these things—
sit alone beside desert figwort
      tiny, purple, orchid-like;
employ no other masters

than heliotropes and *Fagonia indica;*
let *gharaz* be my holy scripture;
become for a day the foliage, leaf,
stem and root of purslane-leaved *Aizoon;*

sprout as exuberantly out of the hard-packed
drifted sand—I earn my keep
as the desert creatures' high priest.
When I settle for a while at my still point,

gaze intently enough to notice the ripple
in the dewdrop collected on one leaf
of *Fagonia ovalifolia,* grasp how it regards me
in its own way, believe it hears what I say,

I ride the wind—play it
with as much finesse as dunes play
the *shamal*—my spirit soaring
with desert lark, dashing here and there

---

1. From Wendell Berry's book, *The Unsettling of America: Culture and Agriculture* (1977)

with the grounded francolin.
And though I've longed to be caught up
into swirling galaxies, I beg,

      Please leave me to succumb
      to desert squash and red thumbs.

The Carrot Family

Umbelliferae

Here's the secret to thriving

in this desert: taking part in the life

of lady's lace—glabrous herb

sprouting in cultivated land. Listen

intently till you hear the lower leaves

of each bishop's weed withering at anthesis.

Though you be heavy, notice

how each fruiting umbel opens

as if in flight. And though darkness

appears to reign, how each one—

long-peduncled—reflects one ray

of mysterious, glorious light.

Mint and Nightshade Families

Lamiaceae and *Solanaceae*

Here and now, Vernal Equinox,
the desert greens: intricate branches
of Egyptian sage sing in depressions;

buds in the spillage of sewage promise
to burst forth any day now from umbrellate
short-peduncled corymbs of black nightshade.

Wait
      with caper white,
neither of you doubting,

till worm moon—
              poised between crescent and full—
reveals each flower's opening
before dawn.

Come drift   among four-angled stems
of sages and germanders, the silvery aspect
of the small-spined silverleaf nightshade,

many-seeded berries and flowering stars
of desert thorn—abode of jinn[1]—
painting the desert red and violet.

---

1. Refers to the Middle Eastern and African thought that spirits
   inhabit desolate places

Linger
          among native shrublets
                in shallow places,
                      in coarse-soiled depressions,
                            among perennial herbs on hamadas,
                                  in runnels and *wadis*,
                                        on rocky slopes.
Come,

let's hang out among hairy nightshade,
weed of disturbed and enriched places
lavishing its graces equally on sewage pond
and tended garden
                (may we do likewise).

Let's meditate on herbs and low shrubs
growing in rhythm—the instant's incarnation.

Let's enter into each herbal presence,
    each tangle of white fleece in narrow runnels,
        each shrublet a bridge,
            each broad-leafed herb a juncture,
                each rigid thorny plant a channel
                    to the other side.

Overhead,
          the jubilant song of a desert lark.
And at our feet,
weeds blossoming.

So tired of playing god,
    let us be a mercy for all nature.[1]
Wild-scented desert,
    herb and weed-enriched,
let us love you without judgment,
    with absolute abandon.

---

1.   Refers to Qur'an 21:107

Snapdragons and Black Mangrove

Scrophulariaceae and *Acanthaceae*

Forget playing it safe.
If you need mentors to show the way,
employ climbers and twiners,

or thistle-like spiny ones—volatile
fragrance wafting from spike-like racemes
or cymes in axils of upper leaves.

Scrawled across desert sands, secrets
of the universe dispersed by dawn
and evening breeze. Be bold

as desert figwort flourishing among rocks
and stone fragments. Be spiny-tipped
and prickly-toothed as the eyelash plant,

braving gravelly habitats—
slight rises and shallow runnels,
both portals to the other side,

unfolding in liminal spaces, sprouting
in gaps, breaking through cracks
in the desert's pavement, reproductive urge

throbbing in their calyxes and corollas.
Find yourself in the core of their bracts.
Keep still long enough to get caught up

in a moment of being—bold as these herbs,
at one with sand and wind, moth and bee,
tender parched earth. Whirl like a dervish

round and round, joyfully unraveling yourself
from every fantasy of safety. You with these
herbs—figwort and black mangrove—

in the theatre of desert space, the grace
of *sabhkas*, swaying in the *shamal*,
full of life, your feet sprouting wings,

all fear of flying forgotten as you elevate
and float light as a desert lark's feather
above the climbers and twiners.

Broomrape Family (Prayer for Herbal Benefits)

Orobanchaceae

Cistanche tubulosa

sanctify me

Your fleshy stem covered

    with oblong-lanceolate scales

        save me

Your ovoid fruit

        fill me with love

Your thick dense spike

        strengthen me

Your calyx with acute

    scarious-margined lobes

        empower me

Robust perennial root parasite

        hear me

Within your littoral salt marshes

    hide me

May I never be separated from you

    Protect me by your yellow blue purple

      flowers from evil's power

Call me dear desert hyacinth

    at my death's hour

Plantain Tribe

Plantaginaceae

The sparingly hairy herb ispaghula
flourishes on fine deposits

in depressions. The densely
silken-haired herb wedaina

enhances sandy southern habitats.
Buck's-horn plantain—pinnately cleft

with acute lobes—creates basal rosettes
on compact alluvial soil. Lancelike

ribwort's leaves taper to a petiole.
So may my soul

rise up out of harsh aridity
into the silence shunned

by the world, starburst
of earth's truth, quantum leap

into the space between
depression and sky, safe

from insecticides, far
from manicured lawns.

May my soul catch fire
from the bee just now honing in,

honing in
on one corolla,

on one corolla,
heaven under its feet.

Daisy Family (The Essence of Inflorescence)

Compositae or *Asteraceae*

The *Compositae* live as if
my garden is heaven.
They sustain themselves
through drought, feign to live
on when my life's played out.

Sitting still   as a frog   rock-sunning,
I observe how their flowers crowd
into heads on a common footstalk.
Choosing them for friends, I meander
with them along the muddy path

between the world's veracity and void,
note their brief peak—rays and discs—
day by day the sun harsher, see
how their filaments are free,
anthers united, some leaves armed

with thistles, others not: *Aaronsohnia*
daisy   mugwort   white thistle
with leathery leaves   field marigold
perennial thistle   knapweed (cobwebby herb)
chrysanthemum with its naked receptacle

dwarf chicory with bitter milky sap   the prostrate
Eclipta.   In their natural habitat—
depressions of fine-textured sediments,
gravelly soil   alfalfa fields
        borders of irrigation canals—

they bear the lash of sand,
scarcity of rain. No fountain,
no watermill.   Persistent *shamal*.
And yet, what jubilance—all
secluded from industrial pollution.

Every spring blossoming
stunningly, fragile inflorescences
distracting from the yellow-tinged horizon.
Dazzling   humbling   silencing me
as each one hints of transiency.

True Grasses (Pioneers)

Gramineae

Entering the desert without disturbing
one narrow leaf-blade of star grass,
  let questions of science give way
   to humble reasoning and sky meditation—
imagine no pipelines, no oil flares to soil
the air, nothing but aromatic grasses,

vast infinity of lemony *Cymbopogon*
parkeri, marvel grass and hairy crabgrass
   bringing you back to sky mind,
   desert mind, each inflorescence
a sketch of fleeting nature, life's essence.
The silence of goosegrass entering

the heart, its wiry stolen-like stems
sneaking along sandy depressions.
   Creeping lovegrass—its spikelets
   gracefully swaying in the shade
of *Ziziphus* and *Acacia* scrubs.
Vitally present these infinite grasses,

they deserve a toast: sturdy and lucid,
braced against the *shamal*, fluid in alluvial
   and fine deposits, on sand hills,
   in damp fields, in waste moist places
of the *rodat*, in ditches, channels,
sandy depressions. Staring into the sun

without blinking, each tuft and pedicel,
culm and panicle a dreamsong rising up
        toward the cloudless sky. Look
        how honey bees and desert whites come
at their beck and call, how they lift you high
above all the parched, cracked earth to float

on the notes of the desert lark.

Sedges (Steadfast Perennials)

Cyperaceae

When I grow weary traveling this Milky Way

all alone, panic setting in, I go out

to maritime sand or inland gravelly soil,

meander scarab beetle-like among graceful

lilting sisters softening a harsh desert—

praise how they dress themselves

in spikelet clusters, perfume ever so subtly

but sweetly the desert air while masking fumes

from the distant oil flare:

rasha among ruins of a forgotten fishing/

pearling village; smooth flatsedge

lavishing its graces on marshy places;

tuberous bulrush filling in margins where

water spills—runners of its creeping

rhizomes dilated in woody tubers.

Perennial herbs assuaging my rage

touched off by the latest tragedy—

earthquake on the remote Tibetan plateau,

children trapped in collapsed schools

built by the Chinese, while purple nutsedge

sends its long slender stolens bearing black

tubers and leaf rosettes along the moist ground.

Sacredness of the commonplace.

Graceful, lilting sisters softening this harsh

desert no human invaders built,

the only minarets in sight, their prostrate

rhizomes kissing the ground,

their flowers in dense heads or glumes

the only gold domes around,

dominating this airy space.

Back in the city, in the cold sterility

of MegaMart, my eyes smart

as I wonder if I could live

on the trigonous nut of *Cyperus*

conglomeratus—spare myself

this weekly trip. Among *Cyperaceae*,

dance and throw my grocery list away?

How could I ever again live apart

from sedges and the desert lark,

its song urging each

creeping

        rhizome

                on?

Thilooth (Tactic of Succulence)

Halocnemum strobilaceum

The fifteenth choice of Qatar's annual
"A Flower each Spring" campaign, 2014

Finally, its turn has come.
    After fourteen years,
it's having its day in the sun—
    thilooth, the flower of the hour,

thriving in littoral salt marshes,
    a halophyte putting up a notable fight
against excessive salinity—succulent
    leaves diluting salts absorbed from soil.

Not at all showy—in fact,
    an undershrub—with minute
yellow flowers grouped
    together, forming dense spikes.

Its scientific name a poem
unto itself (say it slowly):

Hal	*oc*	*ne*	*mum*
stro	*bi*	*la*	*ceum—*

a rhyming couplet. *Sabat*,
jointed glasswort its common names.

Come with me to Al Khor,
    to Abu Samrah, to the coastal *sabkha*
east of Dukhan ridge where
    camels and gazelles graze it

intensively on playas of fine silt,
    on chalky sands of excessive salt.
Observe how it thrives
    in its saline-tolerant clique

among opposite-leaved saltwort,
    mangrove grass,
    string of beads,
    glaucous glasswort.

Who could not help but love
    this halophytic undershrub,
so richly branched, its tri-
    clustered flowers flawless—

possessing both stamens and pistils—
    its leaves little bud-like knots
along each stem. Let *thilooth*
    take you in—lead you

to the desert's edge; let it beg you
    not to intrude, to weigh
the cost of its loss. Let it
    comfort you as the chaotic,

imperfect world closes in—
    see it taking a stand,
recolonizing oil-polluted marshland,
    holding back the sea with its petite

        flowers come autumn.

Wildflowers over the Sand-sea

In the desert, everything and nothing
        to lose, I take my clues from wildflowers.
                Hoping not to be nibbled on, I head

for a sandy *wadi* to learn Syrian rue's
        secret—why seldom grazed.
                Then on to *tumba* to investigate

how it can spread so far and wide,
        lying prostrate in hard sand.
                Wishing to learn the knack

of not needing a firm foundation,
        I seek out desert pink—
                that succulent herb I've heard

thrives in drifted sand.
        Desiring to find what's needed
                just in time, I turn to deep pink

conoid catchfly, which always
        manages to find a damp nook.
                Needing to devise a way to keep

predators at bay without being vicious
        about it, I inquire of blooming
                Centaurea sinaica how to grow

those creepy soft prickles that cause
        nothing but harmless tickles.
                Wanting always to be a beacon of light

even in the darkest night, I look
    for desert campion in the dunes
        to ask how to flower after dusk.

Seeking to foster hope in the midst
    of death and decay, I take a lesson
        from magenta-floraled sea lavender

on fossil corals. Hoping always to soften
    hard hearts, I find spider flower
        among rocks, shining orange as the sun.

Then knowing days will come
    when I'll need a weapon to ward off
        the aggressor, I go to deep blue

eyelash plant to ask how to be
    more dangerously prickly.
        I go with specific requests, but

each one knows best what I need—
    each flower undeterred by austerity,
        offering communion to a drifting pilgrim.

Hispid Herbs

When Ali Sharif watered the thirsty Arabian
primrose, and I shrieked, That's our last bottle!
he didn't say a word—simply smiled
while his eyes clearly implied,
Why survive if we let *kahal* die?
Every shallow sandy deposit a mosque,
each herb a godly word nourishing
parched hearts with its very being.

Powdery red dust rubbed off thick roots
once used by Bedouin women for rouge.
Small hispid bristly herb, its lemon-yellow
flowers attracting desert leopards
December to April. Who could remain
double-minded, hesitating between God
and the world, refusing to praise as the Prophet
flower takes center stage this exotic hour,

teaching how to thrive in drearily dry
conditions? Today, beside this sandy
depression—charmed by Arabian primroses,
silenced by fluty notes of a Persian nightingale,

sensing I'm still effusively alive—
I acquiesce to sun and wailing *shamal*,
the soothsayer desert lark in the air
divining my future. And I wonder
how they'll survive—the desert
city's asthmatic children who never
reach out their hands to touch
the white bulbous-based bristles

on the leaves of a hispid herb,
    who haven't heard
    how the earth—paved over—
    gasps   for   air.

Bitter Apples

Citrullus colocynthis

All day clouds hung over the desert.   All day wind blew as if to brew a great storm of hard long rain.   But once again, nothing came of them. Beside a *wadi*, I waited—endured hunger and heat, slept among bitter apples: *colocynth* thriving on sandy loam, its perennial root sending forth scabrid vine-like stems. Solitary yellow flowers bloomed in the leaves' axils. Lemon-sized gourd-like fruit was filling up with soft white poisonous pulp in which flat ovate seeds would eventually please birds of passage who'd stop over to disperse them. I lifted the discarded tin can off one trailing vine so it could continue to climb across the desert floor. Unable to resist, I tore one from the ground to transplant in my garden. But its delicate microscopical leaf structure caused it to wither within an hour. Clouds still hanging low, wind continuing to blow, I recalled how its fruit flourished profusely between Palestine's mountains and the Mediterranean's eastern shore, Gaza to Mt. Carmel—soil and climate all-sufficient for its growth. I took note: Leave things where they grow. Wild gourd of the Old Testament[1]—earth gall, exceeding bitterness—and yet, its nutty-flavored seeds taken from their poisonous enclosure, innocuous. In hard soil, widespread. Desert Bedouins grind and make a bread. Precious food source of one Central Saharan tribe—Tibboo Resade—seeds trampled on to remove the last traces of bitter pulp, cleaned by winnowing, mixed with ashes from camels' dung, placed on a smooth stone and rubbed with another to crush the testa, kernels sifted, boiled in water, dried in the sun, then mixed with desiccated powdered dates till finally palatable, nutritive. This is how we live: tearing through the toxic enclosure to what can sustain us.

---

1.   Refers to II Kings 4:38–40 (Holy Bible, KJV)

Gourds and Parasitic Herbs

Cucurbitaceae and *Cynomoriaceae*

When I catch myself speculating about
sanctity, recalling Mother Theresa's words,
Holiness is not a luxury reserved for the few,

but an obligation for us all, I go out to sit
awhile among trailing herbs and leafless
root-parasites. What holiness,

what freedom beyond fear.
Sound of dew dissipating off bristles,
deeply lobed leaves, congested flowers,

tendrils entangled in the *shamal.*
Dewdrops—water's sacredness—stoking
the fires of desire for living life fully.

The coiling, sprawling perennial herb
vine-of-Sodom, bitter gourd—
prostrate on sandy, compact soil,

its bitter fruit dried and sold in folk
pharmacies as laxative, cure for snake
and insect bites, joint pain reliever, hair dye;

its ripe fruit once used for gun powder.
The bristly prostrate perennial herb
globe cucumber on gravelly soil,

containing purgative properties.
The fleshy leafless perennial herb
with congested flowers: Maltese mushroom

parasitic on chenopods of maritime sands
and salt marshes, *Tarthuth* its Arabic name—
an aphrodisiac in Bahrain,

destitute of chlorophyll, its reddish-
brown spadix club-shaped.
Inspired for the flame,[1] desiring

transformation, I celebrate the sacredness
of Mother Earth's gifts—rhythms,
seasons, fruitfulness. I note

her vulnerability to the addicted
consumer, slave of the marketplace.
Incited, inflamed by a tendrilled herb

and a phallic red thumb,
beholden to them, I become
that light substance, winged and sacred,[2]

my selfhood fading into illusion.
Commingling with these herbs, I come to be
one with the sum of all created things.

---

1. "Want the change. Be inspired by the flame where everything
   shines as it disappears." —Rainer Maria Rilke, *Sonnets to Orpheus*,
   Part Two XII
2. Plato's definition of the poet

Fervor of the desert renewing faith
in flora's supreme power, liberating news
of herbs, I rant beside fragrant holy runnels

and depressions. Safe from young
aspiring capitalists, I pass the time
with bejeweled scarab beetles.

Don't wait till it's too late to care,
I plead, though no one's there to hear.
Species going, going, gone.

Soon from these Arabian waters,
the gentle dugong. Soon from
this desert's heart, these holy herbs.

Leadworts and the Gentian Family

Plumbaginaceae and *Gentianaceae*

Come into the saline habitat not to escape
your own species, but to encounter them
and Gaia as well, all things full of Her—

each dewdrop a holy anointing
of sea lavender and lesser centaury.
In salines along the coasts,

on beaches and *sabkha* edges,
that halophytic low shrub—
Qataf, the natives named it—

thriving, its fleshy leaves secreting salts,
its minuscule flowers housed in a naked
terminal panicle, blooming March till May.

In moist habitats, the annual glabrous herb,
Branched centaury, stiff-stemmed,
the whole of it a lax flat-topped cluster

of inflorescence, naturalized weed.
You will need no sweeter place
to lie down once stars appear. You,

with your dusty feet, could entrust yourself
to a peaceful sleep there among
sea lavender and lesser centaury.

You would awaken into joy
and reunion, free from the idolatry
of money and rampant greed.

Finally flourishing in, of all places,
the desert's heart—fertile ground producing
not only growth and blossoming of

leadworts and gentians, but your own
rebirth. You would disappear to spurt
into something new that masters your earthly form

as you pour yourself out like a stream.
Stay till the dawn's crest swallows the moon.
Romantic love a deceiver, you turn now

and forever after to the brown earth
that's graced you with a second birth.
On sun-drenched salines beside irrigation canals

full of bully common mynahs,
melodious white-cheeked bulbuls,
ubiquitous quarreling sparrows

drinking and eating their fill,
pray for the children of this land as they inhale
petroleum's by-products more deadly

than the banned elixir of fine
spirits and wine. Ask sea lavender
and lesser centaury to save them.

Yet in August

Torn between the trellised and untrellised,
I praise plants from the Holy Qur'an,
cultivated fruit trees—date palm,
pomegranate, olive,
fig, ginger, grape,
Christ's thorn;
plants from the Hadith and Sunnah—
Camel's hay, citron,
orfot and true senna.

Praise plants that bring me face to face
with creation, resurrection.
Yes, praise beet and kust.

Praise annuals—the cultivated:
onion, leek, and garlic;
mustard and sesame;
safflower and wheat;
rice and barley; lentil
and black cumin.

Praise creepers and climbers:
melons; pumpkins; gourds.

Praise wild perennial herbs:
"heart of the desert" ones like Bitter gourd;
aquatic ones—wild ginger, cust root,
sweet flag, Narrow-leaved cattail, saffron.

Praise cultivated perennial herbs:
aloe, sweet basil. Praise desert shrubs:
toothbrush tree and salt tree;
cultivated shrubs henna and katam.

Praise wild desert trees: acacia,
umbrella thorn, tamarisk.
Praise tropical/subtropical trees:
camphor, kamala, banana.

August gardens overflowing,
shamal winds blowing
over the arid desert landscape.

Mirages like mirrors.
Heat rising like incense
from the desert's heart.
Dormant seeds
waiting for winter rains.

Beyond the tended garden,
not a hint of green. Austere grace
of a barren waste. One Crested lark
cries out against stark reality.

But oh the sound one dormant seed can make
splitting open hard-packed ground,
exposing parched earth's intimacies.

Yet in August, redemptive winter rains
seeming most improbable.

Once the Salubrious Winter Winds,

like the wave of a fairy's wand,
transform the landscape into a mosaic
of pastel flowers, one must admit

    this desert's not so desolate after all.
    Focus your attention on just one tree,
    you'll see what I mean: Acacia

tortilis perhaps, that umbrella thorn,
leguminous with fragrant luminous
clusters of yellowish white flowers—

    four hundred on a single branch,
    flourishing where rainfall may be merely
    forty millimeters a year.

Consider its value: forage and shade
for the grazers; pods fed to lactating
animals to increase their milk;

    honey from its blossoms; medicine
    from its seeds, bark and leaves.
    I would be so useful.

Don't you hear it?
the tree's direct link—urgent call
to the soul's predawn:

    Humanity, I give you
    my divine self—my roots
    laid deep in this Arabian Desert.

In return, I yearn only for respect—
the primitive satisfaction
of setting seeds in spaces between
stones of the desert's pavement.

Lean forward, if you will,
into my frame of mineral mind:
inhale my sweet scent.

Take up this chant.

The Twenty-Two Most Mentioned Plants in the Qur'an

Manna

Terfeziaceae, Tamarix gallica, or *Acacia erioloba*
Qur'anic: *al mann*; Arabic: *turanjabin* or *kazanjbin*
Qur'anic reference: 2:61

Was it the desert truffle,
all these three thousand years
known to be edible,

or the sweet gum from the tamarisk tree,
insects—*Coccus manniparus*—
puncturing the bark,

releasing the saccharine exudate?
Or was it Camel's thorn?
Or perhaps simply the name

for all strange nourishment
the Israelites found during exile[ii]—
manna meaning *what is it?* in Hebrew.

Today is it the Kurdish manna,
produced from a desert shrub,
Haloxylon salicornicum?

Dried sap, or honeydew excreted
by bugs who eat the sap?
Point is no matter what it is or was,

manna came and was obtained
without struggle or strain,
keeping humans alive to thrive

and tell their story. Glory
be to the Sustainer of all life,
Creator of all matter and manna.

Alhagi maurorum, "Manna"

Date Palm

Phoenix dactylifera
Qur'anic: *nakhl*; Arabic: *balah*

The righteous shall flourish like a palm tree.   —Psalm 92:12, NKJV

...lofty date palms...   —Qur'an 50:10

Plant mentioned more often than any other
in the Qur'an, *Phoenix dactylifera*,
cultivated eight thousand years ago
in Mesopotamia, perhaps the only fruit
domesticated at that time, with golden-
layered spathes enclosing dates,

named after the mythical bird,
its uses numbering the days in a year.[1]
Placed in mouths of newborns,
served at weddings and to begin and end
each day of Ramadan. Let me always
keep one leaf of it within reach,

a stash of its fruit in my cupboard.
Dioecious by nature, the male capable
of pollinating one hundred females.
Its fruit a demulcent, emollient,
heart stimulant, memory loss deterrent,
laxative, diuretic, aphrodisiac.

Fiber- and potassium-rich. Such
an impressive list of essential nutrients,
vitamins, minerals, antioxidants!

---

1. Ancient Arabic adage

Phoenix dactylifera, "Date Palm"

I shall eat seven every morning—
if not the Ajwa from Medina, then
the Khalas from Qatar's Umm Bab,

to protect me from poison and magic,
as one Hadith suggests. King
of the oasis, whose drupe fruit is thin-
skinned, soft-fleshed and succulent.
Six hundred varieties. Imposing
and elegant, featured in poems of Arabia,

Africa, Egypt, Homer, Chaucer,
Shakespeare. Now here.
Archonthophoenix—from the Greek
archon: a chieftain, phoenix.
The stately date palm begins, remains
six to seven years as a little bud,

vulnerable tuft of leaves at ground level.
From the crown's center, its single
growing point, emerge leaves
among which pale green buds appear.
Lovely when left to their own devices—
suckers from the base a grace of a fountain

of greenery around the trunk,
its branches once used to greet Jesus.
Waving them, the people chanting,

> *Hosanna, blessed is*
> *the King of Israel.*[1]

———————————

1. John 12:13 (Holy Bible, KJV)

Olive

Olea europaea
Qur'anic/Arabic: *zaitun* or *zaitoon*

*Also a tree springing out of Mt. Sinai, which produces oil
and relish for those who use it for food.* —Qur'an 23:20

Blessed by sunrise and sunset,
belonging to the whole world,
neither of the East nor of the West,[1]

it is our best ambassador for peace.
Spreading from Phoenicia, northern
Arabian Peninsula, throughout

the Mediterranean to Australia,
New Zealand, Palestine, South
Africa, California, Chili.

Short and squat, its trunk typically
twisted, it would never be listed
among the majestic ones—Giant

sequoias, California redwoods.
Though no match for the magnificent
magnolia, its small flowers—cream-

colored—are fit for a fairy queen.
Gnarled yet graceful, wandering
branches silver-sprayed—symbols

---

1. Qur'an 24:35

of peace (the dove with its twig),
glory, abundance—used to crown
victors of wars and games.

In its small drupe of a fruit, an oil—
marvel of antioxidants, nutritious demulcent,
laxative, emollient for skin and massage.

Delectable oil for salads and cooking,
obtained from a *blessed tree*[1] the Prophet
advised to use for food and massage.

Nothing wasted. Leaves for remedy.
Wood for crafts and carpentry.
Blessed be the ones, human and machine,

crushing, extracting the oil.
Lower be my cholesterol, stronger
my muscles, slower my aging

as I partake. But may I take note:
at the opposite end from where the golden
liquid emerges, *billions of bitter*

little nubbins[2]—oleo-rubin.
Lastly, that luminescent property
of its oil: *Light upon light.*[3]

---

1. A hadith from Dārimi, 69:103
2. Zwingle, Erla. "Olive Oil: Elixir of the Gods." *National Geographic* 196 (1999): 66–81.
3. Qur'an 24:35

Close your eyes. Fantasize:
You're in a grove of sacred olive trees.
A hot breeze enlivens the leaves—

silver-green foliage heavy with fruit,
yet feather-light with the flute-like
liquid song of a Persian nightingale.

Grape

Vitis vinifera
Qur'anic/Arabic: *inab*

...and grapes from which you derive intoxicating
drink, but also good nourishment. —Qur'an 16:66–67

Second most often mentioned plant
in the Qur'an,[1] perhaps originating
in Armenia or Azerbaijan,

then spreading to Arabia, Egypt, Iran.
Today, ten thousand varieties.
Included among the holy ones—

with fig, palm and pomegranate.
Once, visiting Napa Valley,
I yearned to buy a small vineyard.

Passing it every day,
noting it had fallen into disarray,
I'd say to the unkempt vines,

If you were mine, I'd dress you
with care so divine you'd think
you'd been transplanted

into the Garden of Paradise,
or returned to Eden. I'd let
your fruit dry into luscious raisins

---

1. A total of eleven references

fit for the Prophet's cup,
seeped in water till the tonic
could be drunk.

Sad to say, I couldn't afford
to buy that forsaken vineyard.
To this day, I visualize it

each time I savor
a grape or raisin,
and I wish...

Pomegranate

Punica granatum
Qur'anic/Arabic: *rumman*

Mentioned merely three times in the Qur'an,
but to be found in Paradise.[1]
Beneath its shiny, leathery rind,
a myriad of cell-like juicy sacs.
Symbol of fertility and immortality.

Its crinkly scarlet flowers once gracing
Babylon's Hanging Gardens. Ancient
Egyptians entombed with them.
Persephone, accepting one single seed
from one aril, condemned to spend
a part of each year in the underworld.

Native from Iran to the Himalayas,
cultivated for millennia, migrating as far east
as China, found along the Silk Road.
Depicted on the walls of the royal palace
and fortress Alhambra, Islamic Nasrid Dynasty.

Oh, to grow such a shrub in my garden—
its flowers to relieve my sore eyes,
its fruit to soothe my nerves, refresh
my brain, improve my appetite.

---

1. Qur'an 55:68

Will no one ever again say of my cheeks
they are *like halves of a pomegranate
behind your veil?*[1] Unlikely, since they've
grown a bit hollow and saggy.
But at last I've learned to live
with a vengeance, the pomegranate
my latest for-instance. At leisure,

I cut gently into one, pry open six sections
with pleasure, ease away seeds from peel
and membranes, then munch away.
But may I not let the *slow flames of {God's}
lovely produce fall into ashes.*[2] Jewels,
red and precious edible rubies,
may I suck each sweet-tart sac with joy.

Punica granatum, "Pomegranate"

---

1. Song of Solomon 6:7 (Holy Bible, ESV)
2. Rainer Maria Rilke, "Growing Old"

Fig

Ficus carica
Qur'anic/Arabic: *at-tin*

By the fig and the olive and the Mount of Sinai, and this
City of Security (Mecca)—We have indeed created man in
the best of moulds.   —Qur'an 95:1–4

Fig tree, how long it's been full meaning for me.
    —Rainer Maria Rilke, "The Sixth Elegy," *Duino Elegies*[iii]

Fig tree of heaven, leaves of which
covered Adam's and Eve's bodies.
Small and cultivated in poor soil, the only
tree chosen to name a Qur'anic chapter.

Fruits produced only on trees tiny hidden
agaonid wasps burrow into to fertilize, then die.
Plato's favorite fruit, so much so that
people called him Philosokos: *lover of fig.*

Ficus carica, "Fig"

First and last tree cited in the Bible—
Genesis and Revelation. Invisible
flowers flourish on fleshy funnels'
inside walls, which swell around pips,

becoming the fig—each one
a heaven-offered gift. Lift
your eyes from the void to see
fig and wasp in perfect harmony.

Dream of paradise as you slice
through indigo skin, but take note:
the meeting of eternal and ephemeral
as you taste the fruit.

Plant this one singled out with olive
and pomegranate as Allah's blessings,
allowing its roots minimal rambling space.
Late summer, forage for ripe figs

among heavy leaves. When joints
become arthritic, make this request:
Bring me wrinkled purple figs from it—
and cream cheese, please.

Cedar

Cedrus libani or *Ziziphus spina-christi*
Qur'anic/Arabic: *sidr*

From the face of the mountain, the cedars raise aloft
their luxuriance.   —Epic of Gilgamesh (3,000 B.C.E.)

Some say this is the tree of eternity,
lote, marking the utmost boundary
of human knowledge.[1]

Some say it's Lebanon's cedar.
Arz al-Rab or Shajaratul-Allah,
Tree of the Lord.

Mentioned frequently in the Bible,
Cedars of Lebanon.[2] Solomon's temple
and palace built of its scented timber.

Arabia's most beautiful tree,
with its terraced effect,
pyramidic when young.

The biblical Erez (Hebrew),
Arz (Arabic), Cedrus (Semitic).
Sidrah. A tree of Paradise...

---

1. One hadith says: "There everything that comes up from earth
    stops, and it is taken from there; and everything that comes
    down stops, and it is taken from there...The tree at which the
    knowledge of every prophet...and every angel stops."
2. Psalms 104:16

amid thornless lote trees.[1]
They say perhaps when cedar
became scarce in Lebanon and Syria,

juniper took its place till it, too,
was disgraced, then *Ziziphus*[2] was chosen
because it grew prolifically in Arabia.

The Prophet said, *Watering Sidr*
is equal to giving water to a thirsty believer.[3]
A noble timber with a handsome grain,

resistant to decay, its fragrance enduring.
So much to gain by keeping company with it.
We drove to see the grove of true cedars

up Mt. Lebanon's slopes, Bsherra,
burial place of the poet Gibran.
Four hundred great trees—descendants

from which King Solomon built his temple.
Spice-scented limbs drew me in.
I zeroed in on one young female cone

protected by a cluster of yellow-green needles.
Years later, southeastern Turkey's Taurus
Mountains, I marveled at the sight:

---

1. Sarat al-Waqi'a 56:28 (Qur'an)
2. *Ziziphus spin-christi*
3. Another hadith says the Prophet warned: "All those who would
   cut *Sidr* will be sent to Hell with their heads down."

largest natural woods of Lebanon cedar
surviving. I heard them sighing
for their home—gnarled, storm-battered,

one thousand years old, clinging to slopes
of the Taurus. Oh to meander among cedars
like a day moth in and out of their shadows—

inhaling, exhaling, trailing swallows back
to the barn, my arm laden with a hint
of heaven-scent resin, ever grateful,

my life enriched by the gift. From the Epic
of Gilgamesh, to the Bible and Qur'an,
to Egyptians using cedar resin to embalm...

to the cross of the crucified Christ,
its majesty and longevity
a symbol of eternity.

Tamarisk

Tamarix aphylla
Qur'anic: *athl*; Arabic: *tarfa*

One of three survivors, 542 A.D.,
great flood of Yemen's kingdom
of Saba. Common tree or shrub
of peninsular Arabia, Africa, Eurasia.
Considered a weed, an invasive
species in the U.S. and Australia.

Roots twenty feet into the ground.
Evergreen, flowering in winter.
Capable of thriving in the most difficult
environments—tolerant salt cedar
of high-salinity soil. Only tree
found on the shores of the Dead Sea.

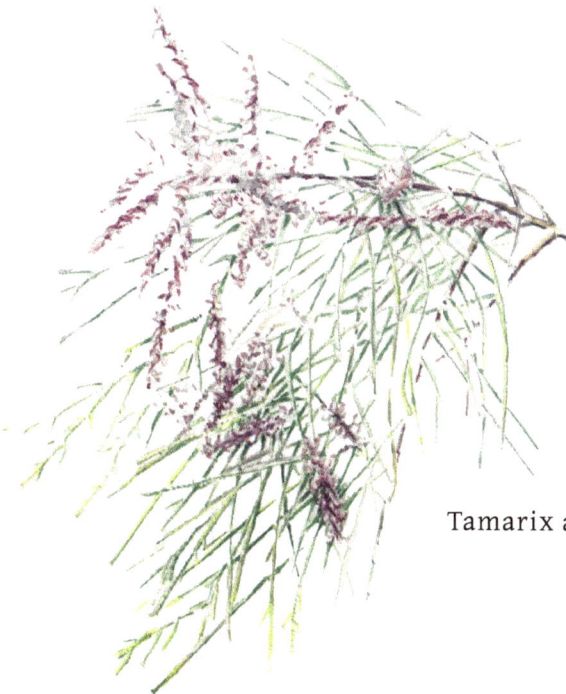

Tamarix aphylla, "Tamarisk"

In the Qur'an, it denotes a degraded
environment: ... *replaced their gardens*
by two others bearing bitter fruit,
tamarisks and stunted lote trees. [1]
But Old Testament Abraham
planted one to honor God. [2]

Sturdy tree of bitter fruit, yet fit
for the King of kings. Survivor,
a thriver. One to emulate, meditate
upon. With each new flood,
to pause and applaud the tamarisk,
to be star-struck by its clever tenacity.

Entering the space of a tamarisk,
to let oneself risk becoming one with it—
every inch of its brilliance. Glimpse it
from a distance for perspective's sake,
then come up close: take
in every detail. But keep silent

as a Cistercian monk. So much wisdom
in its twisted, furrowed trunk—listen:
scales of leaves whispering in the breeze.

---

1. Qur'an 34:16
2. Genesis 20:33

Toothbrush Tree

Salvadora persica
Qur'anic: *khamt*; Arabic: *miswa* or *arak*; Urdu: *peelu*

The Prophet said, *Were it not for my fear*
of imposing hardship... I'd have made it
a duty to miswak five times a day before prayer.[1]

When Mohammed Ali's wife, after lunch
one day, gave me the gift of a miswak stick,
I felt myself slip into the culture.
Putting away my Colgate[iv] Total,
I opted for local brands with extracts
from *Salvadora persica*—Miswak
Plus from Saudi, Siwak-F from Bali,

Epident from Egypt. Fennel flavor so divine,
clear link to the sublime. From that time,
I became obsessed with finding the tree
in the wild—in sandy loam, on rocky slope.
With resolve and hope, I set out desert-bound,
sniffing for the scent of cress or mustard.
Climbed every hillock, descended
into depressions in search of it. I admit

I was distracted once or twice by desert
hyacinths and campion. But still
I sought the champion of healthy teeth
and sharper mind. I took my time—
mouth watering for a mystifying,
clarifying wonder twig. Miswak:

---

1.   A hadith, one of the Sayings of the Prophet

chewing stick of Arak. A pre-Islamic
custom, Islamized by the Prophet 543 A.D.
Arabia's valued tree of berries and leaves
tasting peppery, roots and twigs
with salts and resins that clean and shine.
So many attributes: whitening teeth;
firming gums; enticing appetite;
improving vision and memory.

Finally, pure joy as I chewed,
my breath and mind imbued
with terrestrial, celestial thoughts.

Salvadora persica, "Toothbrush Tree"

Henna or Camphor

Lawsonia inermis or *Cinnamomum camphora*
Qur'anic/Arabic: *kafur*

Is it the white, transparent solid
with a strong, aromatic scent,
or a moth repellent, embalming fluid,

ingredient in Indian food? Or is it that
for which traders since sixth-century C.E.
called at Sumatra's western coast?[v]

Thirteenth-century price of camphor equal to gold.
Barus, famous city of camphor,
forgotten now, its precious trees

sacrificed for timber. Visualize
the crystallized terpene ketone,
now synthesized from turpentine.

Or is it copher to which Solomon[1]
compared his beloved—henna,
Lawsonia inermis, Egyptian privet,

commonly found in Arabia and Egypt?
Semitic, *hinna*; Greek, *kufros*.
In the Qur'an, *kafur*, which is

hinna, not Indian *kapur*
(camphor), to be sure.
Confusing, yes? But let's reflect:

---

1. Song of Solomon 1:4

henna's perfume is used in cosmetics;
its flowers and leaves cast a red hue
one might attribute to wine;

pre-Islamic Egyptians applied it
to the dead; one Hadith advises,
and last of all, sprinkle Kafur.

Lawsonia inermis, "Henna"

From Japanese to Javanese,
camphor trees are quite exquisite.
But are they what the Prophet meant

when he spoke of Kafur?
Who can say? It's rather unclear,
but one thing's for sure,

Verily, the righteous shall drink
from a wine cup tempered at the
Kafur fountain.[1]

Why not salute all three—[2]
each tree a gift of God—because
by the sea or deep in the desert

they survive, their gold crystallized
at the appointed hour—that fifth decade—
wizened roots seeped in deep darkness.

Let the steadfast Camphors and Hennas
be today's tonic and perfume, tomorrow's
embalming fluid as you're entombed.

---

1. Qur'an 76:5
2. *Lawsonia inermis, Cinnamomum camphora,* and *Dryobalanops*
   camphora

Ginger

Zingiber officinale
Qur'anic/Arabic: *Zanjabil* or *Zanzbil*

And they will be given to drink there of a cup
(of wine) mixed with Zanjabil.   —Qur'an 76:17

Endemic to India, dried
and imported by Arabs of old,
rhizome of a perennial herb,

Zingiber officinale
now renowned.
Ginger bread and beer,

snaps and pastries,
curries and condiments,
medicine since ancient times.

A gift basket of ginger was sent
from the *Ruler of Rome* to the Prophet,
one Hadith says.

I would be the inferior one—
small and white, spicy enough
for Asian dishes—or red and rich

in atsiri oil for medicine. I'd be
the tablespoonful added to a child's
first batch of gingerbread men.

I'd be the bit that a mother adds
to the tea she and her daughter sip
while sharing a secret dream or regret.

I'd gladly wear two hats—spice
and herbal cure. Bring me, please,
one rhizome with several buds

so I might plant and harvest them
for spice and medicine. Then, alas,
may I be offered that promised drink.[1]

Zingiber officinale, "Ginger"

---

1. Qur'an 76:17

Lentil

Lens culinaris
Qur'anic/Arabic: *adas*

In ancient times, the poor
used lentils to make bread,
the rich used wheat.

Four varieties, the red
most popular. At every meal
in Nepal, I ate *dhal;*

my digestive system and heart
content. Composed of twelve percent
water, sixty percent carbs,

twenty-five percent protein.
Regrettably causing flatulence,
an expense I'll gladly pay.

Must we crave variety and meat,
always wanting more till finally,
death at the door, we long

for simple pleasures once enjoyed?
Among legumes, one makes a plan
to give up rich foods and take a stand

with vegetarians, live modestly
as once imagined, welcoming
the gift of lens-shaped seeds hidden

in pods on a bushy annual plant—
sumptuous bounty rich in carbs,
proteins, minerals,

fiber and Vitamin B1.
With a bowl of lentils,
I sit and scan a wheat field

in the distance, grateful
at this instance to be poor,
alas, once more.

Onion

Allium cepa
Qur'anic/Arabic: *basal, thom,* or *soom*

More than sixty varieties are grown
Arabia and Egypt. Ancient Egyptians
worshiped and swore by them.

The Israelites, wandering
forty years in the desert,
yearned for them.

Sliced and diced, chopped and liquidized,
dried and flaked or powdered,
onions are prized for foods and medicines.

But the Prophet advised not to enter
the mosque till the smell
on the breath had dissipated.[vi]

Good for all that ails—from baldness
to boils, common cold to toothaches,
insect bites to hepatitis, earaches

to headaches—another miracle cure.
Considering onion—rich source
of flavonoids offering fortification

from cancers, heart disease,
inflammation—one understands
how even the glands of some plants,

blissfully watered in gardens,
were created for our well-being.
Pity the one who cannot lose herself

in wonder over the marvels of an onion—
its layers like those of the universe,
how it protects from insects,

keeps unwelcome guests
out of one's face.
Bearing in mind the Vidalia

(that pioneer of all sweet onions),
onion rolls, fried onions,
the corner hot dog stand with its relish

Allium cepa, "Onion"

and onions as condiments—
it only makes sense
to praise the onion.

Let me loosen the soil,
make space in my kitchen garden
among radishes and runner beans

for this precious gift from God.
When you're on the brink, and you think
it's time for a heart scan,

or you're waiting for results
of the biopsy, stand at the kitchen sink,
peel the onion under a trickle

of water, little trick passed
from mother to daughter,
to keep the eyes from tearing.

Garlic

Allium sativum
Qur'anic: *fum*; Arabic: *thum*

Belonging to the lily family,
officially a vegetable not herb,
relative of onion and chive.

Known as Poor Man's Treacle—
Theriac, "heal all"—ancient
Egyptians thought it nearly a god.

Remedy for many ailments,
containing antioxidants.
Good for everything from asthma

to cholera, hypertension to nasal
congestion, paralysis to typhus.
Of antibiotic value.

Its methanol extract a rich
source of flavonoids
to protect human health.

Builders of the Pyramids ate it.
Old country remedy for whooping cough:
a garlic clove in the whooper's shoes.

Two hadiths reveal the Prophet
was repelled by its smell—instructed
those eating it not to enter the mosque

till the odor had left the breath.
Every kitchen garden should include them
among tomatoes, marrows, potatoes.

Let me treasure my trove of garlic cloves—
come early spring, take one bulb,
break it apart, plant each clove

in light, well-composted soil
in a sunny place, one-inch deep,
six inches apart. Then late summer,

leaves dried down, lift each bulb
from the ground, and with love
hang up in a dry place among small

bunches of marjoram flowers,
thyme and fennel stalks. Now
let me rub my salad bowl

with one sliced clove, take four more
and make a creamy taramasalata
for my bread and black olives.

Cucumber

Cucumis melo
Qur'anic: *Qiththa*; Arabic: *Khiyar*
Qur'anic reference: 2:61

Cucurbits grown since ancient times,
Arabia and Egypt: pumpkin, water and
muskmelons, gourds and cucumbers.

Ah, the cooling properties
of cucumbers—promising relief
from spicy heat. What it lacks

in nutritional value, it makes up for
with its cooling effect. Just yesterday,
I begged for some in yogurt—

the Indian dish too hot.
One hadith indicates the Prophet
ate fresh dates and cucumber together.

Containing no saturated fats,
no cholesterol. Protects against
colon cancers. Source of potassium.

Its peel good dietary fiber—no more
than the forest's reflection, a green so
pure it feels like a revelation.

Perhaps in old age, I'll have a glassed-
in greenhouse, or a hothouse equipped
with a stove and hot air flues to force

cucumbers out of season. What a gift
they'll be in my outdoor garden
once spring's shadows lift.

Like a hidden glen
between steep granite slopes,
a vegetable-melon gem.

Gum Arabic Tree

Acacia nilotica
Qur'anic: *Talh*; Arabic: *Sunt Garath* or *Tulh*

It shall be the reward for Heaven's people.   —Qur'an 56:27–33

. . . one whiff . . . is all Arabia   —Rudyard Kipling

Eating ice cream and candy,
I give thanks for the acacia—
for its gum arabic. I come

into the shade of one
in the desert and praise
its slanted, flat top; admire

its wisdom: small leaves
for conserving water;
thorns and prickles keeping

grazers at bay; the heartwood's
deposits of metabolic wastes
serving as preservatives—

making it unpalatable
to abrasive insects, resistant
to invasive fungi.

Sole wood used to construct
the tabernacle and all its features.
Chosen by Noah for the ark,

by boat builders in ancient Egypt
and modern Sudan. We are broken,
out of sync with the universe

while the acacia's not strayed
one millimeter from the sacred way.
Listen: Persian nightingale still singing

plaintively dawn and dusk
from its crown. A haunt
from the beginning till now

for little owl *Athene noctua*,
Crested lark, Southern Grey
shrike and White wagtail alike.

Acacia's austere stamina
resonates with the hermit's resolve.
Perhaps it's no match

for the Scotch fir. Still,
I would prefer its solitary stand
against persistent grains of sand.

In its presence, poisons
hovering on the horizon
fade to an illusion.

Gourd

Lagenaria siceraria
Qur'anic: *Yaqtin*; Arabic: *Yaqtin, Qarat,* or *Dabba*

*...we caused to grow over him a spreading plant
of the gourd kind.*   —Qur'an 37:146

When Jonah (Prophet Yunus) was cast out
from the whale's belly, he had the gourd[vii]
to thank for sustenance and shade

from scorching sun. Yaqtin, Bottle
or Calabash gourd. Bottle squash
grown in Arabia since ancient times.

Some say it's a kind of pumpkin.
Hairy, fast-growing, trailing or climbing
annual herb, its large yellow flowers superb.

Huge smooth leaves for shade
rustle flies away while its fruit provides
good nourishment: rich in essential

minerals, iron, protein, trace elements,
fiber to dispel digestive orders.
Delicate nutty flavor delectable

with hot curries, cooling yogurt dishes.
Eat it like squash; it has a crisper texture.
One hadith says the Prophet said,

Let them eat gourd, for it
stimulates intellect and brain.
Another hadith says *heart.*

Let me grow Bottle gourds in my
kitchen garden—when I suffer from
insomnia, mix its juice with sesame oil.

And if I'm ever cast up on a *naked shore*[1]
spewed out from some whale's belly,
may God send a gourd to sprout and ascend

over my head—to nourish and protect
as surely as Jonah's did, remind me daily
how God provides and forgives

when we disobey. How could a heart
be ungrateful or ever again unfaithful
after the gift of the gourd?

Jonah survived to tell of the herb
sent on his behalf from above.
What greater love?

---

1. Qur'an 37:145

Mustard

Brassica nigra
Qur'anic: *Khardal*
Qur'anic references: 21:47 and 31:16

We shall set up scales of justice ... if there be no more
than the weight of a mustard seed, we will bring it to account.
   —Qur'an 21:47

The kingdom of Heaven is like a mustard seed ... grown,
it is the greatest of shrubs and becomes a tree.
   —Matthew 13:31–32, NRSV

Metaphor for the smallest sin.
Annual herb grown in Arabia,
Africa for edible seed oil.

One hadith says, *Whoever has pride*
as little as a mustard seed will not
be allowed to enter Paradise.

Garden vegetable, well-known condiment.
Spectacular displays of white flowers
early spring. Yes, let's introduce it

into cultivation—the latest sensation!
Collect leaves before plants flower,
sauté in olive oil with lemon juice.

A seed so small can do it, but us?
To possess such faith to face all odds?
We're so full of caution and regret;

how can God expect so much from us?
But to grow is existence. Ask any plant.
With its humble persistence, it keeps

breathing, roots reaching down
and up and out, setting new seeds.
Nothing random or wanton about it,

leading us closer to the blessed
unknowing, following God's mandate
to a tee—fruiting and multiplying,

replenishing the earth, thus protecting it.

Brassica nigra, "Mustard"

Sweet Basil

Ocimum basilicum
Qur'anic: *Ar-Raihan*; Arabic: *Rehan, Habaq,* or *Hook*
Qur'anic references: 55:12–13; 56:89

*The Prophet said, "Do not refuse a gift of Rehan because
it is from Paradise."*   —Hadith[viii]

Found wild and cultivated
throughout Arabia, its provision
described as God's gift and favor.

Known in Iran as shahasparam,
king of herbs, and nazbu,
plant with a delicate scent.

Highly fragrant, popular culinary herb,
source of essential oils for flavoring foods,
ingredient in dental products and fragrances.

A European pot herb with superb
curative value. Roots used as balm.
Good for everything from anxiety

to Aromatherapy, arthritis
to bronchitis, insomnia to hysteria,
hepatitis to multiple sclerosis.

Its leaves offer a scent of cloves.
Seeds soaked in water: a refreshing
Mediterranean sherbet tokhum.

Half-hardy annual, a delicate plant
best grown under glass, as alas it needs
heat to release its clove-like flavor.

Sow seeds late spring. If no hothouse,
choose sunniest garden spot, or grow
in a pot or window box on a sunny sill.

Ideal, as well, for scented gardens.
Herb of contradictions and predictions—
devil's possession or remedy against witches?

Must I curse, as Greeks and Romans did,
as I sow, to ensure germination?
Poisonous or not? Could just a whiff of it

breed a scorpion in my brain? Insane
notion! But so a French physician
once claimed. Ah, sweet basil

in my pasta sauce, beans and salad.
Give me one tablespoon freshly chopped
to sprinkle over a pound of sliced tomatoes,

one teaspoon to mix with garlic,
oil and grated cheese to spread
over pizza dough, please.

Tonic and natural tranquilizer,
increasing concentration, let me inhale,
imbibe and bath in it

against fatigue and anxiety.
May its essence infuse me with everything
herbalists and aromatherapists promise.

Let me sneak a pot into my sick friend's
room so she might breathe in its aura—
her shining knight in green armor.

Ocimum basilicum, "Sweet Basil"

Euphorbia

Euphorbia resinifera
Qur'anic: *Az-Zaqqum;* Arabic: *Rijlat-Iblis* (vegetable of Satan)
Qur'anic references: 17:60; 37:62–68; 44:43–48; 56:52–55

The tree of Zaqqum will be the food of the sinful, like molten brass!
It will boil in their insides.   —Qur'an 44:43–48

Tree of Hell providing poisonous
food for sinners. Thorny
plant with a bitter taste.

Shajr al-Maluna,[ix] *cursed tree*
causing burning in the stomach;
stems like demons' heads;

highly toxic latex gum,
yet important medicine
from Greek Galen's time.

In Arabia, many species—
all poisonous, full of thorns,
fruits small and useless—

yet none known as *Zaqqum.*
So which of several hundred
is the Qur'anic one?

Moroccan *Euphorbia resinifera,*
whose stems clubbed in a round shape
truly resemble a devil's head?

Farooqi[x] concludes yes.
Others think it's *Balanites aegyptiaca,*
colocynth, or *Euphorbia abyssinica.*

Whichever it might be … *it is a tree*
that springs out of the bottom of Hell fire:
the shoots of its fruit stalks like devil's heads. [1]

Mere simile? Nothing of God's creation
worthless? Tree of Hell one hundred
times more sinister than *Euphorbias?*

Like Judas trees of Judea, saddled
with the legend—Iscariot hanging
himself from one after betraying Jesus—

must *Euphorbias* carry such a burden?
Let's make of them merely a warning
while esteeming their healing properties.

Bless them while preparing to avoid
the fire, their presence shining light
on the choices between wrong and right.

---

1. Qur'an 37:62-68

Thorn

Qur'anic: *Dhari*

*No food will there be for them, but a bitter Dhari, which will
neither nourish nor satisfy hunger.* —Qur'an 88:6–7

The Bitter thorn: flip side
of the Plenty's Horn.
No food for sinners in Hell.

Cactus perhaps,
or a thorny grass,
more bitter than aloes.

Seaweed, some propose.
Others *hanzal, Citrullus
colocynthis.* Imagine:

eating and never being filled—
hunger never sated, growing
more and more malnourished.

Food bitter as medicine
sticking in the craw like pricks
of a pin to the skin.

Yet the greatest pain:
remembrance of all the food
once enjoyed, even manna

once provided in the desert.
Olives and dates,
pomegranates and grapes,

figs, ginger, onions, garlic,
cucumber, mustard,
sweet basil, the gourds.

And the glorious trees:
cedar, tamarisk, toothbrush,
camphor and acacia.

The legumes, lentils.
Even the plant *Euphorbia*,
with its curative benefits—

how it could quench the fire
the Bitter thorn will cause.
Ultimate punishment: kept alive

but hunger never satisfied,
barely to survive, yet to realize
you didn't make it into paradise.

Those trees of life taken for granted
forever off-limits, their dazzling magnificence
burned into your consciousness.

Never to be pardoned and permitted
into the garden. Stuck on the side of death
from which you'll never resurrect.

No more gathering of loved ones
to eat of earth's bounty—lentils,
veggies, fruit. You've been given the boot.

Ousted. Exiled.
No chance of a mistrial.
To call "Allah, Allah,"

yet know He'll never hear you
above the crackling of the flames.
To ache for escape from haunting

scents and craving tastes.
But you must wait
forever. It's too late.

Blessed Tree

Qur'anic: *Tuba*

For those who believe and work righteousness, Tuba is
for them and a beautiful place of [final] return.
      —Qur'an 13:29

The Prophet said, "There is a tree in whose shade a rider could
travel for a hundred years without crossing it."
      —Al-Waqi 'ah 56:30 (Hadith)

Tuba is a tree in Paradise one hundred years big. The
clothes of the people of Paradise are made from its calyxes.
      —Ibu Hibban (Hadith)

Ethiopian word, *tuba*,
synonymous with paradise.
Majestic, tall and shady.

Perhaps another name
for cedar, *sidr.* [1]
Amid thornless lote-trees.

Or is it similar to Syria's
walnut, *al-Jawzah*, as Imam
Ahmad's hadith suggests?

Best timber and best of all nuts,
Juglans region. Not at all showy,
its leaves the last in spring to bud,

---

1.   Qur'an 34:28

first in autumn to fall sulphur-brown.
But its wood the most beautiful
color and patterns of graining.

Long history of cultivation—long
as the fig's—from Persia to Greece
to Roman Empire, *Jovis glans*:

Juniper's acorn. Circassian walnut
(Persian, English), reaching ninety feet,
long leaves, broad rounded head.

Wherever you live—near a walnut,
cedar, or sidra, come into its shade:
let its pristine beauty fill

your emptiness, its leaves breathe
renewed life into your lungs.
Climb the rungs

of its limbs with your soul
as a gesture of expectancy—
all that awaits you in Paradise.

Alone in dark green shade—
equipoised between earth and heaven—
worship however you please—

possibly whirling dervish-like
in a summer breeze.
Levitate with joy. Meditate

on the purity of the God-given tree
made for you and me. But not
for us alone—home and sustenance

for butterflies and moths,
squirrels, birds and bees. Stay
stone-still once you've whirled

into ecstasy. Let the tree's gift
of shadowed light ignite your soul
with visions of paradisiacal delight.

Epilogue

For Ali Sharif, Wildflower Expert

A yellow dwarf radiates photons
onto Earth, and impeccably tailored

flowers unfold their petals
like the oppressed unfurling flags

in protest against hunger
and poverty, but mostly

against desperation.
Magnanimous wildflowers,

theirs the most unsordid act
of the day. Don't interrupt.

Let them have their say,
after which you may well decide

silence is the only
appropriate reply.

Endnotes

i. (Title Page) For a discussion of the translation plants vs. planets, refer to this website: http://www.islamicstudies. info/tafheem.php?sura=**55**; scroll down to 55:6

ii. (92) Israelites in exile/desert Sinai complained about manna, longing for the food of Egypt (Holy Bible, Numbers 11:5–6).

iii. (104) "Fig tree, how long it's been full meaning for me,
 the way you almost entirely omit to flower,
 and into the early-resolute fruit,
 uncelebratedly thrust your purest secret.
 Like the tube of a fountain, your bent bough drives the sap
 downwards and up; and it leaps from its sleep, scarce waking
 into the joy of its sweetest achievement. Look,
 like Jupiter into the swan."
 —Rainer Maria Rilke, "The Sixth Elegy," *Duino Elegies*

iv. (111) *Salvadora Persica* has been effectively used since the time of the Babylonians, some seven thousand years ago, for cleaning teeth and keeping the gums healthy. Colgate's scientists have now successfully prepared the extract of *miswak* and blended it with other ingredients known to whiten teeth and freshen breath.

v. (113) For a detailed debate about the confusion surrounding these two, refer to M. I. H. Farooqi's *Plants of the Qur'an*, pages 41–48.

vi. (120) This is from one hadith, *Sayings of the Prophet*. Qur'anic reference: 2:61; Biblical reference: Numbers 11:5–6.

vii. (129) The Bible says it was a caster tree (*Kikayan, Ricinus communis, Palma Christi*) that shaded Jonah.

viii. (133) Tirmizi: 3021; Book 43, English vol.5; Book. 41, Hadees no. 2791; http://www.tib-e-nabi-for-you.com/rehaan.html

ix. (136) See *Plants of the Qur'an* by M. I. H. Farooqi. http://www.irfi.org/articles4/articles_5001_6000/zaqqum_in_the_light_of_quran.html

x. (137) author of *Plants of the Qur'an*

Glossary of Plant Names

Latin to Common

Aaronsohnia factorovskyi: Faktorowsky's Aaronsonia
Abutilon indicum: Indian mallow
Acacia ehrenbergiana: desert acacia
Acacia tortilis: umbrella thorn
Acanthaceae: black mangrove
Aeluropus lagopoides: mangrove grass
Agriophyllum minu: star grass
Aizoaceae: iceplant
Aizoon canariense: purslane-leaved aizoon
Althaea ludwigii: mallow, Ludwig's marshmallow
Ammi majus: lady's-lace, bishop's weed
Angiospermae (Dicotyledoneae): dicot
Antirrhinum majus: snapdragon
Arnebia hispidissima: Arabian primrose, prophet flower (common name in Arabia)
Artemisia vulgaris: mugwort
Arthrocnemum glaucum: glaucous glasswort
Asteriscus: daisy family
Atractylis carduus: white thistle, yellow distaff-thistle
Avicennia marina: mangrove
Belenois aurota: caper white
Blepharis ciliaris: eyelash plant
Bolboschoenus glaucus: tuberous bulrush
Calendula arvensis: field marigold
Calligonum comosum: red arta
Capparis spinosa: caper plant, caperbush, Flinders rose
Centaurea pseudosinaica: starthistle
Centaurea sinaica: knapweed
Chaenactis glabriuscula: sand buttons
Chrysanthemum coronarium: chrysanthemum or mum
Cichorium pumilum: dwarf chicory, wild endive
Cirsium arvense: perennial thistle, creeping thistle
Cistanche tubulosa: desert hyacinth
Cistus or *Cistaceae:* rock-rose
Citrullus colocynthis: bitter apple, bitter gourd, desert squash

Cleome arabica: spider flower
Cocculus pendulus: moonseed
Compositae or *Asteraceae:* daisy or sunflower family
Corchorus trilocularis: wild jute
Cymbopogon commutatus: incense grass
Cymbopogon parkeri: one of the true grasses, of the Gramineae family
Cynomorium coccineum: red thumb
Cyperaceae: sedge
Cyperus conglomeratus (Cyperaceae): sedge, perennial sedge, *rasha*
Cyperus laevigatus: smooth flatsedge
Cyperus rotundus: purple nutsedge
Daucus carota: carrot
Dichanthium annulatum: marvel grass
Digitaria sanguinalis: hairy crabgrass
Eclipta prostrata: false daisy
Eleusine indica: goosegrass
Ephedra foliata: shrubby horsetail
Eragrostis hypnoides: creeping lovegrass
Fagonia indica: of the caltrop family or *Zygophyllaceae* (no common name)
Fagonia ovalifolia: desert squash
Glossonema varians (edule): blooming milkweed
Gramineae: true grass
Gymnospermae gnetopsida (Ephedrales): jointfir
Halocnemum strobilaceum: jointed glasswort
Halopeplis perfoliata: string of beads
Haloxylon persicum: white saxaul
Helianthemum lippii: rock-rose, frostweed
Heliotropium curassavicum: heliotropes
Juncus rigidus: sea rush
Lamiaceae: mint
Leptadenia pyrotechnica: broom bush
Limonium axillare: sea lavender
Lycium shawii: desert thorn
Malva: mallow
Malva parviflora: cheeseweed
Mesembryanthemum nodiflorum: Egyptian fig marigold, slenderleaf iceplant
Mollugo cerviana: thread-stem carpetweed
Neurada procumbens: thorn rose, creeping thorn rose
Oenothera stricta: sand primrose
Orobanchaceae: broomrape

Panicum turgidum: turgid panic grass, desert grass
Papaver syriacum: desert poppy
Peganum harmala: Syrian rue
Pennisetum divisum: bristlegrass
Phoenix dactylifera: date palm
Phragmites australis: common reed
Plantaginacceae: plantain
Plantago coronopus: Buck's-horn plantain
Plantago lanceolata: ribwort
Plantago ovata: desert Indianwheat or ispaghula
Rhamnus cathartica: buckthorn, purging buckthorn
Rhanterium epapposum: no common English name
Rumex dentatus: toothed dock, Aegean dock
Salsola soda: opposite-leaved saltwort
Salvia aegyptiaca: Egyptian sage
Salvia officinalis: sage
Scrophularia deserti: desert figwort
Seetzenia lanata or *Seetzenia orientalis:* no common name
Sesuvium sesuvioides: desert pink
Silene conoidea: conoid catchfly
Silene villosa: desert campion
Solanum elaeagnifolium: silverleaf nightshade
Solanum nigrum: black nightshade
Solanum villosum: hairy nightshade
Solanaceae: nightshade
Sporobolus arabicus: Arabian drop-seed grass
Tamarix ramossissima: saltcedar, five-stamen tamarisk, five-stamen tamarix
Terfezia: desert truffle
Teucrium: germanders
Tilia: linden
Tribulus terrestris: devil's thorn
Typha domingensis: cat's tail
Umbelliferae: carrot
Ziziphus mauritiana: jujube
Ziziphus mucronata: buffalo thorn
Ziziphus rugosa: wild jujube
Ziziphus spina-christi: Christ's thorn jujube, sidra
Zygophyllaceae: bean caper
Zygophyllum quatarense: bean caper
Zygophylum simplex: simple-leaved bean caper

Common to Latin

Aegean dock: *Rumex dentatus*
Arabian drop-seed grass: *Sporobolus arabicus*
Arabian primrose: *Arnebia hispidissima*
bean caper: *Zygophyllum quatarense*
bishop's weed: *Ammi majus*
bitter apple: *Citrullus colocynthis*
bitter gourd: *Citrullus colocynthis*
black mangrove: *Acanthaceae*
black nightshade: *Solanum nigrum*
blooming milkweed: *Glossonema varians (edule)*
bristlegrass: Pennisetum *divisum*
broom bush: *Leptadenia pyrotechnica*
broomrape: *Orobanchaceae*
Buck's-horn plantain: *Plantago coronopus*
buckthorn or purging buckthorn: *Rhamnus cathartica*
buffalo thorn: *Ziziphus mucronata*
caper white: *Belenois aurota*
caperbush or caper plant: *Capparis spinosa*
carrot: *Daucus carota*
cat's tail: *Typha domingensis*
cheeseweed: *Malva parviflora*
Christ's thorn jujube: *Ziziphus spina-christi*
chrysanthemum (mum): *Chrysanthemum coronarium*
common reed: *Phragmites australis*
conoid catchfly: *Silene conoidea*
creeping lovegrass: *Eragrostis hypnoides*
daisy: *Asteraceae (Asteriscus)* or *Compositae*
date palm: *Phoenix dactylifera*
desert acacia: *Acacia ehrenbergiana*
desert campion: *Silene villosa*
desert figwort: *Scrophularia deserti*
desert grass: *Panicum turgidum*
desert hyacinth: *Cistanche tubulosa*
desert Indianwheat: *Plantago ovata*
desert pink: *Sesuvium sesuvioides*
desert poppy: *Papaver syriacum*
desert squash: *Citrullus colocynthis* or *Fagonia ovalifolia*
desert thorn: *Lycium shawii*

desert truffle: *Terfezia*
devil's thorn: *Tribulus terrestris*
dicots: *Angiospermae* or *Dicotyledoneae*
dwarf chicory (wild endive): *Cichorium pumilum*
Egyptian fig marigold: *Mesembryanthemum nodiflorum*
Egyptian sage: *Salvia aegyptiaca*
eyelash plant: *Blepharis ciliaris*
fagonbush: *caltrop family*
Faktorowsky's Aaronsonia: *Aaronsohnia factorovskyi*
false daisy: *Eclipta prostrata*
field marigold: *Calendula arvensis*
five-stamen tamarisk or five-stamen tamarix: *Tamarix ramossissima*
Flinders rose: *Capparis spinosa*
frostweed: *Helianthemum lippii*
germanders: *Teucrium*
glaucous glasswort: *Arthrocnemum glaucum*
goosegrass: *Eleusine indica*
green bristle-grass: *Setaria viridis*
hairy crabgrass: *Digitaria sanguinalis*
hairy nightshade: *Solanum villosum*
heliotropes: *Heliotropium curassavicum*
iceplant: *Aizoaceae*
incense grass: *Cymbopogon commutatus*
Indian mallow: *Abutilon indicum*
ispaghula (desert Indianwheat): *Plantago ovata*
jointed glasswort: *Halocnemum strobilaceum*
jointfir: *Gymnospermae gnetopsida* or *Ephedrales*
jujube: *Ziziphus mauritiana*
knapweed: *Centaurea sinaica*
lady's lace: *Ammi majus*
linden: *Tilia*
mallow: *Malva* or *Althaea ludwigii*
marvel grass: *Dichanthium annulatum*
mangrove: *Avicennia marina*
mangrove grass: *Aeluropus lagopoides*
mint: *Lamiaceae*
moonseed: Cocculus pendulus
mugworts: Artemisia vulgaris
nightshade: Solanaceae
opposite-leaved saltwort: *Salsola soda*
perennial sedge: *Cyperaceae* or *Cyperus conglomeratus*

perennial thistle or creeping thistle: *Cirsium arvense*
plantain: *Plantaginacceae*
prophet flower: common name (in Arabia) for *Arnebia hispidissima*
purple nutsedge: *Cyperus rotundus*
purslane-leaved aizoon: *Aizoon canariense*
rasha: *Cyperus conglomeratus*
red arta: *Calligonum comosum*
red thumb: *Cynomorium coccineum* or *Fagonia ovalifolia*
ribwort: *Plantago lanceolata*
rock-rose: *Helianthemum lippii*
sage: *Salvia officinalis*
saltcedar: *Tamarix ramossissima*
sand buttons: *Chaenactis glabriuscula*
sand primrose: *Oenothera stricta*
sea lavender: *Limonium axillare*
sea rush: *Juncus rigidus*
sedge: *Cyperaceae* or *Cyperus conglomeratus*
shrubby horsetail: *Ephedra foliata*
sidra: *Ziziphus spina-christi*
silverleaf nightshade: *Solanum elaeagnifolium*
simple-leaved bean caper: *Zygophylum simplex*
slenderleaf iceplant: *Mesembryanthemum nodiflorum*
smooth flatsedge: *Cyperus laevigatus*
snapdragon: *Antirrhinum majus*
spider flower: *Cleome arabica*
star grass: *Agriophyllum minus*
starthistle: *Centaurea pseudosinaica*
string of beads: *Halopeplis perfoliata*
sunflower: *Compositae* or *Asteraceae*
Syrian rue: *Peganum harmala*
thorn roses: *Neurada procumbens*
thread-stem carpetweed: *Mollugo cerviana*
toothed dock: *Rumex dentatus*
true grass: *Cymbopogon parkeri*
tuberous bulrush: *Bolboschoenus glaucus*
turgid panic grass: *Panicum turgidum*
umbrella thorn: *Acacia tortilis*
white thistle or yellow distaff-thistle: *Atractylis carduus*
wild jujube: *Ziziphus rugosa*
wild jute: *Corchorus trilocularis*

English to Latin

Baluchistan gerbil: *Gerbillus nanus*
cape hare: *Lepus capensis*
desert lark: *Ammomanes deserti*
desert leopard: *Apharitis myrmecophylia*
desert wheatear: *Oenanthe deserti*
Ethiopian hedgehog or desert hedgehog: *Paraechinus aethiopicus*
false cobra: *Malpolon moilensis*
greater short-toed lark: *Calandrella branchdatyla*
honey badger: *Mellivora capensis*
jird: *Meriones crassus*
lesser Egyptian jerboa: *Jaculus jaculus*
oryx, Arabian oryx, or white oryx: *Oryx leucoryx*
palm dove or laughing dove: *Spilopelia senegalensis*
Persian bulbul: *Pycnonotus leucotis*
Persian nightingale: *Pycnonotus leucotis*
rear-fanged sand snake or Arabian rear-fanged snake: *Malpolon moilensis*
red fox: *Vulpes vulpes arabica*
Rueppell's sand: *Vulpes rueppellii sabaea*
sea bream or twobar seabream: *Acanthopagrus bifasciatus*
white-eared bulbul: *Pycnonotus leucotis*
wind scorpion or camel spider: *Solifugae*

Glossary of Arabic words

alhamdulillah: praise be to God or thank God
gharaz: Cynomorium coccineum
ghasoul: Mesembryanthemum cryptanthum
gurdhi: Cocculus pendulus
hamada: a type of desert landscape consisting of high, largely barren, hard rocky plateaus, where most of the sand has been removed by deflation
hammada elegans: Haloxylon persicum
harm: Zygophyllum quatarense
hazm: stony, gritty; a slight rise between depressions
hureim: Zygophyllum simplex
huwa: Launaea capitata

jafna: Aizoon canariense
jebel: hill or a range of hills
jinn or *al-jinn:* spirits
kahal: Arnebia hispidissima
kamah: desert truffle
khalifah: steward
mistah: threshing floor; a place where dates are dried; an instrument to level something
raqrouq: Helianthemum lippii
rodat: shallow natural depression
sabat: Halocnemum strobilaceum
sabkha: salt flat
shamal: northwesterly wind
sidr: Ziziphus spina-christi
suhaili: southeast wind
thilooth: Halocnemum strobilaceum
thumam: Panicum turgidum
tumba: Citrulus colocynthis
wadi: a dry (ephemeral) riverbed that contains water only during times of heavy rain
wedaina: Cistanche tubulosa
zikr: devotional acts in Islam in which short phrases or prayers are repeatedly recited silently within the mind or aloud; in Islam; the remembrance of God by rhythmic repetition of God's names or attributes

DIANA WOODCOCK holds a Ph.D. in Creative Writing from Lancaster University, where she researched poetry's role in the search for an environmental ethic. In 1974, she earned a B.S. degree in Psychology, and in 2004 an M.F.A. degree in Creative Writing. She has worked as a counselor with delinquent youth, an editor of a young women's magazine, and a teacher of English as a second language. For nearly eight years, she lived in Tibet, Macau, and on the Thai-Cambodian border, teaching and working with refugees. Since 2004, she has been teaching creative writing, environmental literature, and composition at VCUarts Qatar. She is the author of seven chapbooks and six poetry collections, most recently *Heaven Underfoot*, winner of the 2022 Codhill Press Pauline Uchmanowicz Poetry Award; *Holy Sparks*, a finalist for the 2020 Paraclete Press Poetry Award; and *Facing Aridity*, a finalist for the 2020 Prism Prize for Climate Literature. Her debut collection, *Swaying on the Elephant's Shoulders*, won the 2011 Vernice Quebodeaux Pathways Poetry Prize. She is a three-time Pushcart Prize nominee and a Best of the Net nominee. Her poems have appeared in *Best New Poets 2008*, *Women's Review of Books*, *Nimrod*, *Crab Orchard Review*, *Southern Humanities Review*, *Spiritus*, *Comstock Review*, and other journals and anthologies. Her grand prize-winning poem, "Music as Scripture," was performed onstage in Lincoln Park, San Francisco, by Natica Angilly's Poetic Dance Theater Company at Artists Embassy International's 21st Dancing Poetry Festival.

SHANTI ARTS

NATURE ▪ ART ▪ SPIRIT

Please visit us online
to browse our entire book catalog,
including poetry collections and fiction,
books on travel, nature, healing, art,
photography, and more.

Also take a look at our highly regarded art
and literary journal, *Still Point Arts Quarterly*,
which may be downloaded for free.

www.shantiarts.com

www.ingramcontent.com/pod-product-compliance
Lightning Source LLC
Chambersburg PA
CBHW040137270326
41927CB00020B/3430